The Wonderful World of WHEY LOVER'S COOKBOOK

Original recipes using Fortified Whey

A nutritious dairy-derived food.

Susan Dusharme   **Christina Dillane**

Joe Parkhill — Honeyologist

THE WONDERFUL WORLD OF WHEY LOVER'S COOKBOOK

Copyright © 1982
Susan Dusharme - Christina Dillane

Joe M. Parkhill publishes and distributes this New and Unique Whey Lover's Cookbook thru:
COUNTRY BAZAAR
Publishing and Distributing
Route 2, Box 190 • Berryville, Ark. 72616
(501) 423-3131

ISBN-0-936744-08-1

ALL RIGHTS RESERVED

No part of this publication may be reproduced, stored in a retrieval system, or transmitted in any form or by any means — electronic, mechanical, photocopy, recording, or otherwise — without the express prior permission of the authors.

THE WHEY LOVER'S COOKBOOK

— An Outstanding First —

The Whey Lover's Cookbook is a brand new publication of appetizing recipes, recently developed for the use of nutritious Fortified Whey. Cooks and food lovers everywhere are delighted by this useful cooking guide, arranged in a charming presentation of appealing dishes and helpful hints.

This book is designed with your basic needs in mind. It offers recipes to please the palate of the discerning gourmet, yet with a simplicity of style that will encourage the less adventurous of cooks. In easy to read type, it contains helps for those on varied diets and restrictions which are a part of our lives, yet allows a wonderful blend of textures and tastes.

Most preferred cookbooks are not addressing today's health problems, while results of research in modern medicine are turning physicians to dietary control. **The Whey Lover's Cookbook** does provide options for the increasing number of people who need to lower sugar and cholesterol, . . . not to mention the soft and bland dieters. Special symbols identify special recipes, such as those with no eggs, no major dairy products and no flour.

The recipes look familiar. Yet the use of Fortified Whey now adds a unique improvement of tastes and textures that cannot be duplicated with the use of powdered milk.

This book is a well thought-out effort in creating a kitchen tool that earns its place as most used by the busy homemaker. It encompasses the aspects most valued by today's cooks:

- Easy to follow instructions.
- Familiar tastes and ingredients.
- Easy and oustanding recipes to please the most discerning guest.
- Useful for menu planning and spur-of-the-moment dishes.
- Wholesome adjustments for health . . . that don't require major changes in purchasing, preparation, or taste.
- Use of economical ingredients.
- Instructions for making basic mixes . . . for those wanting to economize or reduce intake of commercial preservatives.
- A volume that covers all the bases, provides a well rounded foundation for Fortified Whey use, and still retains its practical size.

Whether you cook a lot, are just learning, have diet restrictions, concerns for better health, or just enjoy good, wholesome eating, **The Whey Lover's Cookbook** holds a surprise just for you.

Remember, as cooks and meal planners, you are more responsible for the health of your household than your family physician.

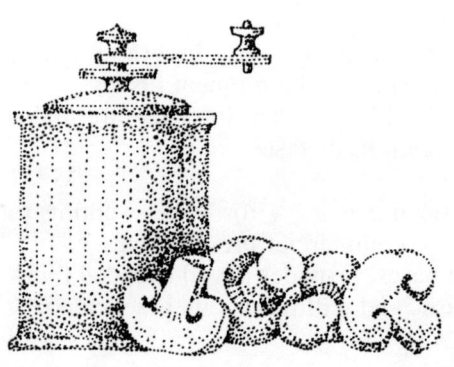

FROM NURSERY RHYME
TO NUTRITIONAL RESEARCH

In 1979, a major breakthrough was made with whey. Highly nutritious, whey is the normally discarded by-product of cheesemaking. Dairy scientists in Utah were finally able to develop a formula that would turn whey into an extremely good tasting dairy drink. Having the appearance of milk, this new Fortified Whey provided the same types of nutrients as Mother's milk, but with many added benefits and surprises of it's own.

JUST WHAT THE DOCTOR ORDERED

Fifty percent of the world's population have digestive problems with cow's milk. Casein, a hard to digest milk protein, and lactose, the natural sugar in milk, are the main culprits. Many more people avoid milk because of its calorie count, its cholesterol level, its animal fat, or its mucus causing effect (casein, again). But in Fortified Whey, the lactose and the calories are reduced by almost half, the cholesterol level is negligible, there is no animal fat, and no hard to digest calcium caseinate . . . the congestive mucus agent. With Fortified Whey, children, adults, seniors, who were unable to tolerate milk products now find themselves eating foods they had never tasted or hadn't enjoyed in years.

Dieters take notice of its low calorie count. Cooks see how it actually improves the texture and volume of baked goods, and how these same goods now stay fresh longer. And because Fortified Whey can be purchased economically and delivered to the door, the budget watchers are ecstatic.

HOMOGENIZED MILK CAUSES HEART DISEASE

Although the American public cut its teeth on the idea that milk is the perfect food, a discovery of major consequence is now toppling the sacred bastion of the frosty glass of milk. Medical research* now indicates that homogenized milk is one of the major causes of heart disease in the United States. The homogenization process breaks down fat molecules in milk. These now minute fat particles act to protect a natural milk enzyme, xanthine oxidase (XO) from the destructive effects of the digestive process. This normally, unassimilated enzyme is now, through homogenization, able to pass through the wall of the intestine and circulate to the heart and arterial tissue. This XO acts chemically to scar the artery walls and heart tissue. The body tries to repair the damage by raising the cholesterol level of the blood and depositing the protective fatty material on the scars. With the millions of Americans having been raised on homogenized milk, it is now no mystery that the U.S. cardiac death rate is the second highest in the world. Finland is the only nation in the world that has a greater death rate attributed to cardiovascular related disease than America. Interestingly, we also find that they are the only nation with a greater per capita consumption of homogenized milk!

*Dr. Kurt Oster, M.D., former Chief of Medicine, Director of the E.K.G. Laboratory, and Chief of Cardiology, Park City Hospital, Bridgeport, Conn., "Atherosclerosis; Conjecture, Data, and Facts", Nutrition Today, November/December 1981. And, supported by Dr. Kurt Esselbacker, M.D. Chairman of the Dept. of Medicine, Harvard University.

THE FACTS ABOUT FORTIFIED WHEY

The discovery of the total benefits of Fortified Whey are making more and more people glad that they are hearing about it now. Today, people are taking a closer look at the foods they have previously taken for granted. The timely breakthrough of the Fortified Whey formula gives tremendous momentum to the utilization of whey and its world-wide potential and application.

As a result of the many qualities and aspects of Fortified Whey, every recipe in which it is used has been lifted to a blue-ribbon standard. The value of this cookbook is based upon the tremendous worth of Fortified Whey.

WHEN FORTIFIED WHEY WAS COMPARED
   with the original product . . . milk, there were several commendable surprises. Fortified Whey had:
- Higher percentages of health promoting whey proteins.
- A presence of yogurt culture particles.
- Less lactose (hard to digest milk sugar).
- Less antigens (allergy causing agents).
- A perfect balance of simple and complex carbohydrates, acting as a time release capsule, rather than adding to "sugar-jolt".
- Absence of congestive mucus effects.
- Markedly lower in bacteria count than commercially produced powdered milk.
- Ability to retain nutritional value for three years in powdered form.
- Absence of need to homogenize, which causes a natural milk enzyme, xanthine oxidase, to pass through intestinal walls and result in scarring of blood vessels and cholesterol build-up.

WHEN FORTIFIED WHEY WAS USED
   cooks were ecstatic! Fortified Whey
- Enhances flavor and texture in cooking.
- Reduces the need for shortening, salt, and sweetener.
- Acts as a dough conditioner in baked goods.
- Mixes without lumping or foaming.
- Requires no pre-mixing for cooking and baking use.
- Makes so many things! Soups, Ice Creams, Puddings, Yogurts!
- Is a key ingredient for biscuit, pancake, cake, pudding and cereal mixes.
- Saves trips to the store because of its long storage life.

WHEY CONTAINS

most of the nutrients found in the original milk. All trace vitamins and minerals, which were in the milk are found in variable concentrations in the whey. When digested, whey has a beneficial effect in normalizing digestive disturbances, such as constipation, dysentery and so forth. Apparently Whey is effective because it promotes the growth of helpful bacteria (e.e. lactobacillus) in the colon.

WHEN THE WHEY IS FORTIFIED

it is first dried, then the vitamins and minerals are added. A vegetable oil is added as a natural preservative and to give body to the end product. A complex mixture of carbohydrates is added to balance and supply the body's need for an energy source. Vanillin is added for flavor.

WHEN CHEESE IS MADE

rennet and lactic acid are added to milk to form a curd. The curd contains the milk protein (casein), butterfat and cholesterol. From the curd the cheese is fermented and shaped. The clear, yellowish liquid which remains after separation of the curd is called whey or milk plasma.

WHEN THE PRODUCT IS MIXED WITH WATER, FORTIFIED WHEY IS

- Close to 30 calories lower than a glass of 2% milk.
- Negligible in cholesterol.
- Absent in animal fat.
- More comparable to "Mother's Milk".

IF A STANDARD COULD BE CHOSEN

for a milk suited to the human body's needs, it would be human milk. Cow's milk is meant to go through four digestions, and put three to four hundred pounds of body weight on a calf in its first year.

A KITCHEN VISIT
WITH THE AUTHORS

As homemakers working with a new fortified whey powder, we realized the need of knowing how to use it. We began to experiment, test, try new ideas, compare and test again. We found astonishing new discoveries. We recorded our findings and can now share the numerous ways to work with this delicious product that so many have grown to love.

As each recipe was tested and each helpful hint was formulated, we strove for efficiency, economy, simplicity, wholesomeness, adaptability and practicality. If the recipe did not "measure up" we did not use it in this book.

This book was designed with your basic needs in mind. It offers help for those on varied diets and restrictions which are a part of our lives and yet allows a wonderful blend of textures and tastes.

Some of the recipes are great for camping or backpacking. You will find a small tree symbol by the title. Some are made without one or more of the following ingredients: eggs, flour, or major dairy product.

These have been especially marked for those who have diet restrictions. Some of the recipes are real time-savers for the busy mother. You will find these labeled with a a time-saver symbol.

The variety of things we are able to do with fortified whey is amazing. The best way to sum it up is this:

    YOU CAN DO IT THE NEW WHEY!

    DRINK IT

        MAKE IT

            FREEZE IT

                COOK IT

                    BAKE IT

Once you've tried and tasted some of the exciting new recipes in this personal volume, you will understand why we call this book **The Whey Lover's Cookbook**. Come join us!

t ················ Time-Saver

🌲 ················ Backpacking and Traveling

🚫d ················ No Major Dairy Products

🚫e ················ No Eggs

🚫f ················ No Flour

POINTERS FROM THE PANTRY

STORAGE

It is recommended that Fortified Whey be stored in a dark, cool place and sealed tightly to maintain flavor and value. It can be stored up to two years. For greatest efficiency, store a moderate amount in a counter-top canister for daily use. We use a small canister with a one-quarter measuring cup inside for small, quick needs. We also use a large flour-type canister, complete with a one-half measuring cup for our larger recipes.

MIXING INSTRUCTIONS AND POINTERS

Fortified Whey mixes much more easily than regular powdered milk, but through experience, we found one of the most efficient ways was to blend about one-third of the amount of water needed (using the hottest tap water) and Fortified Whey in the blender. Then add enough cold water and ice to get the desired result. Remember to give the bottle a little shake before pouring. Fortified Whey also mixes easily in a bottle with a tight-fitting cap. Pour in some very hot water, add the powder and shake well. Then add the remaining water and refrigerate.

USE IN COOKING

More often than we first realized, Fortified Whey can be used straight as a powder as well as in liquid form. This means that there is less of a need to make and store large quantities of pre-mixed Fortified Whey in the refrigerator. Each chapter preface includes helpful hints for using the powder or liquid pertaining to the kind of recipes in that chapter. Each recipe will indicate the form of Fortified Whey to be used.

INSTANT FORTIFIED WHEY-ADJUSTMENTS

To adjust for instant Fortified Whey, simply add $1/3$ more than the amount required in the recipe.

TABLE OF CONTENTS

	Page
Cultured Fortified Whey	1
Beverages	7
Soups	11
Main Dishes	16
Sauces and Gravies	22
Desserts	24
Cakes	24
Cookies	29
Pies	33
Frozen	39
Bread	40
Basic Mixes	46

CULTURED FORTIFIED WHEY

CULTURED FORTIFIED WHEY

Cultured Fortified Whey is a source of good taste and great variety. It is incredibly easy to make and is extremely economical. Once you make your first batch and see the many delicious ways you can use it, you will understand one of the main reasons for this little book's existence.

It is necessary for us to call this cultured Fortified Whey by a name other than yogurt, because it can only be called yogurt if made with milk. Therefore, we have happily coined the name "Yofresh" for this new recipe, Yofresh can be substituted, measure for measure, in all recipes that call for yogurt. When you discover all the wonderful new dishes you can create with Yofresh, you, too, will join the fast-growing family of "Whey Lovers."

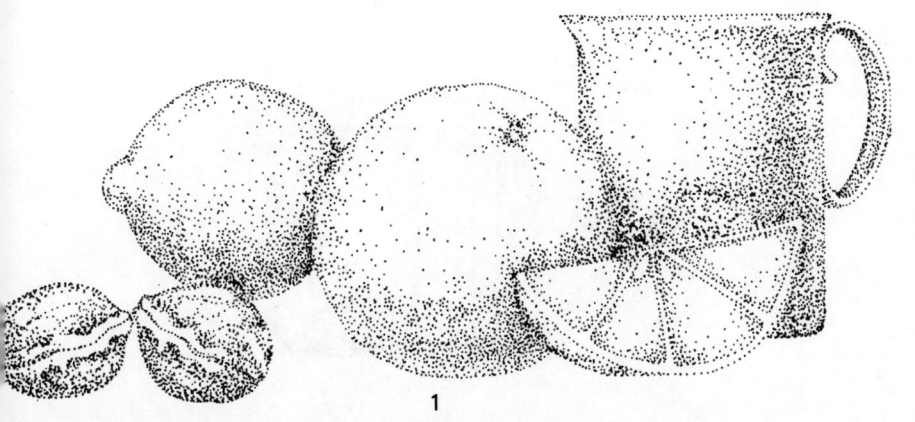

YOFRESH

Our very favorite—and so easy!

1 envelope unflavored gelatin
3/4 c. Fortified Whey powder
4 Tbsp. plain yogurt
Water

1. Sprinkle gelatin on 1/4 c. cold water in blender. Let soften 2 minutes, then add 3/4 c. hot tap water and "stir" for 5 seconds to dissolve.
2. Add 1 c. **warm** water, powder and yogurt to blender. "Stir."
3. Add enough warm water to make 1 quart.
4. Pour into yogurt jars or use any glass jar or bowl with lid. Keep at 110° to 120°F. for ten to twelve hours.*
   *Use a yogurt maker to incubate the Yofresh, or set your oven at lowest temperature for five minutes, turn off, and keep oven door closed for one hour. Repeat every hour. Keep Yofresh in oven the entire time, preferably wrapped in a towel.
5. When time is up, stir Yofresh thoroughly, and chill 3-4 hours in refrigerator to "set-up."
6. Serve with fruit or use in place of yogurt in other recipes.

Variations: After stirring Yofresh add 1-2 Tbsp. of fruit and 1-2 tsp. honey. For vanilla flavor, add 1 tsp. vanilla extract and 1-2 tsp. honey.

Helpful Hints: If you are Yofresh lovers, double the recipe and use mayonnaise jars or any ceramic crockpot and make it in your oven. Then you will have plenty of Yofresh in your refrigerator to use for beverages, cooking and just plain enjoying.

Save 4 Tbsp. of Yofresh to start your next batch.

"CREAM CHEESE" HINT

Try substituting 4 tablespoons cream cheese for the starter in the Yofresh recipe. This makes a delicious, rich-tasting dessert with fresh fruit.

WHIPPED YOFRESH TOPPER

**Gives your fresh fruit or vegetable
platter the zest it needs.**

Place the desired amount of Yofresh in freezer until firm but not solid. Take out and place in blender with 1/4 c. Fortified Whey powder to every 2 c. of Yofresh. Add 1 to 2 tsp. of honey to taste. Blend until smooth and frothy.

CULTURED FORTIFIED WHEY DRINK

**This tastes quite similar to Kefir.
Outstanding!**

1 qt. warm Fortified Whey liquid made with 3/4 c. powdered Fortified Whey
4 Tbsp. plain yogurt

1. Blend or shake Fortified Whey and yogurt.
2. Pour into yogurt jars or covered glass jars and incubate in yogurt maker or oven at 110°-120° for 10-12 hours.
3. Refrigerate until cold, then mix half and half (or to taste) with pineapple, strawberry, apple or other juice.

BASIC YOFRESH SALAD DRESSING

1 egg
1 c. Yofresh
1/2 tsp. dry mustard
1 tsp. onion powder
1 Tbsp. vinegar
1/4 tsp. salt
1-2 tsp. honey

1. Beat all ingredients well and store in refrigerator.

Helpful Hint: Other herbs such as dill, oregano or basil can each be added to get a new flavor for your salads. Use approximately 1/2 tsp. of your favorite herb.

GARLIC AND DILL SALAD DRESSING

Does it taste great over fresh tomatoes!

1 c. Yofresh
1 tsp. dill seed
1/4 tsp. garlic powder
2 tsp. honey
Dash of salt

1. Combine all ingredients in blender and process until creamed. Chill and use as desired.
2. This can also be hand mixed.

LEMON LIGHT FRUIT DIP

What fresh fruit deserves.

1 c. vanilla or plain Yofresh. (p. 2)
1 c. whipped cream
2 tsp. honey
2 Tbsp. lemon juice

1. Mix all ingredients thoroughly.
2. Serve in an attractive dip bowl surrounded by apple wedges, fresh strawberries, orange sections, pineapple chunks or your own creation.

FRESH VEGETABLE DIP

Make this for an after-school snack.

2 c. cottage cheese (whipped in blender if desired)
1 c. Yofresh
1 pkg. dry vegetable soup mix, without pasta.

1. Mix all ingredients and let stand in refrigerator for 2 hours.
2. Serve with crisp vegetables.

ONION DIP

A lo-cal friend at parties.

1 c. cottage cheese
3/4 c. Yofresh
3 Tbsp. onion soup mix

1. Mix and chill.

CLAM DIP

A "must" at get-togethers.

1 c. cottage cheese blenderized
1/2 c. Yofresh
Dash of salt
Dash of pepper
Dash of onion powder
1/2 c. famous thousand island dressing
1 c. minced clams, drained

1. Mix all ingredients.
2. Serve in bowl surrounded by a variety of crackers.

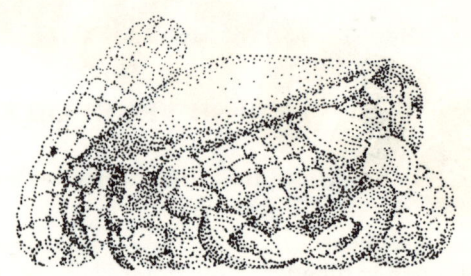

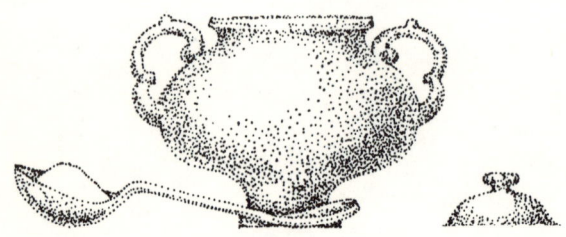

BEVERAGES

BEVERAGES

We all know how delicious a glass of cold Fortified Whey is. And who could say no to a mug of rich, hot Carob Drink*? But were you aware that Fortified Whey powder makes an outstanding shake—in as many flavors as there are fruits! These shakes are very velvety and rich tasting, but wonderfully low in calories.

You can enjoy your own creation when it comes to smoothies. Select your own fruits and juices at the store or use what you have at home. You will be amazed at what you can do with your blender to satisfy your thirst.

Helpful Hints: A spoonful of Fortified Whey makes coffee or tea more enjoyable. Set it out in a small serving bowl with the salt and pepper.

IT'S TIME FOR A "FRESH SHAKE"

2 c. cold water
1/2 c. Fortified Whey powder

1. Blend above ingredients.
2. Add your favorite fruit (banana, peach, strawberries) and 1 tsp. lemon juice, 1 Tbsp. honey and blend until smooth.
3. Add six ice cubes; blend until ice melts.
4. Pour from the blender and drink.

*For a Hot Carob Drink: Warm 2 c. water with 2 Tbsp. unsweetened Carob powder in sauce pan until dissolved and close to simmering. Turn heat off. Stir in 1 Tbsp. honey and 1/3 c. Fortified Whey powder and dissolve. Serve hot!

EASY HOLIDAY EGG NOG

If you've never made egg nog, start out with the best!

1/4 c. cold water
2 tsp. unflavored gelatin
1/2 c. hottest tap water
2/3 c. Fortified Whey powder
2 Tbsp. honey
1-1/4 c. cold or ice water
6 eggs
1 tsp. nutmeg
1/2 tsp. rum extract

1. Pour 1/4 c. cold water in blender. Add unflavored gelatin and let soften 3 minutes. Then stir.
2. Add 1/2 c. very hot water, stir until dissolved.
3. Add powder, honey and stir, then add remaining ingredients. Blend until smooth.
4. Chill.

This egg nog will bring raves and it mixes up quickly and easily in your blender.

WHAT'S UP DOC
IT'S A CARROT SMOOTHIE

2 c. unsweetened pineapple juice
1/2 c. small carrot sticks (about 1" x 1/2")
1/4 c. flaked coconut
1/2 c. Fortified Whey powder

1. Blend all ingredients.
2. Add 6 ice cubes.
3. Blend until ice is melted and serve immediately.

If you like a smoother drink, try using pineapple-coconut juice and omit the flaked coconut. And at your next party, add 1/2 c. of natural lemon-lime soda to this recipe for a delicious new punch!

NEW WHEY SMOOTHIES

Here's your chance to be creative.

1. Take 2 c. of your favorite fruit or vegetable juice.
2. Blend with 1/2 c. Fortified Whey powder.
3. Add a complementary fresh fruit or vegetable if desired (add 1 tsp. lemon juice with fruit). Complementary spices for fruits are cinnamon, ginger, cloves. Complementary spices for vegetables are chili powder, paprika, oregano and parsley.
4. Finish off with 6 ice cubes and blend until ice is melted.
5. Serve immediately and they'll ask for more.

Optional with fruit: 1/2 tsp. vanilla, 1 Tbsp. honey.

Helpful Hint: Complementary fruits include papaya and apricot, banana and strawberries, banana and pineapple, coconut and pineapple and boysenberry and apple.

HOT FRUIT DRINK

While you enjoy your fireplace.

1. Add 1/4 c. Fortified Whey powder to 2 c. of your favorite juice.
2. Stir and heat to just before boiling.
3. Drink hot

Tasty juice suggestions: Boysenberry, pineapple-coconut, apple and cranberry.

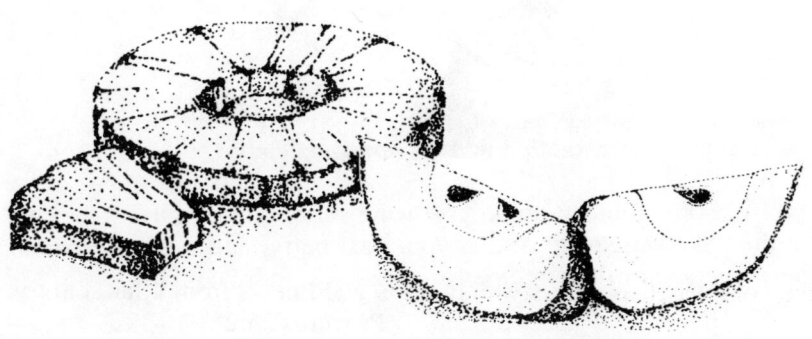

ORANGE-BERRY EYE-OPENER

A quick, fruity way to wake-up your day.

1 c. orange juice
1 good handful of fresh strawberries
1/3 c. Fortified Whey powder
1 egg
1/2 c. water

1. Combine all ingredients in blender and process until smooth. Pour into two tall glasses and serve.

GOLDEN APRICOT SMOOTHIE

An especially nutritious breakfast treat.

2 c. Easy Holiday Egg Nog (p. 8)
1 tsp. lemon juice
1 1/2 c. apricot nectar
2 Tbsp. wheat germ
6 ice cubes (optional)

1. Place all ingredients in blender and process until smooth. Serves 4.

Like cold water to a thirsty soul, so is good news from a far country.
Proverbs 25:25

SOUPS

SOUPS

Fortified Whey powder is a soup maker's delight! It is so easy to "velvetize" your favorite soup by simply adding Fortified Whey powder during the last 5 minutes. And the taste will be better than any you have made before . . smooth and fragrant, like Grandma used to make, but with fewer calories!

HEARTY COD-CHOWDER

Offer a warm "Welcome Home" with this easy dish.

2 peeled and cubed potatoes
1 onion, thinly sliced
1 sprig dill, finely chopped
2 c. water
1 lb. cod fillets
2 c. water
1 Tbsp. butter
1/4 tsp. dried thyme
1/4 tsp. pepper
3/4 c. Fortified Whey powder

1. Simmer potatoes, onions and dill in water in covered pan until potatoes are tender.
2. Cut fish into small chunks, and add to potatoes.
3. Stir in remaining water, butter, thyme and pepper and Fortified Whey powder.
4. Simmer 10 minutes and serve.

Serves 6-8

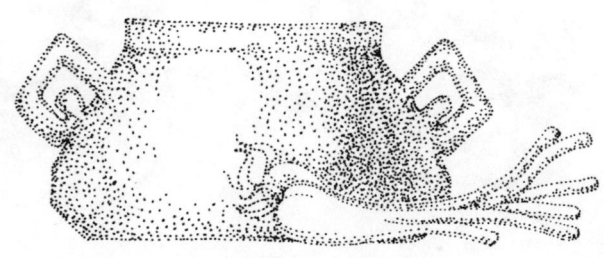

BEST-EVER SPLIT PEA SOUP

Destined to be a family favorite.

1 lb. dried split peas
2 qts. water
2 stalks celery, cut in half
2 carrots, cut in half
2 green onions, chopped
1/2 tsp. thyme leaves
1/2 tsp. marjoram or oregano
Dash of garlic powder and cayenne pepper
1 Tbsp. bacon-flavored bits
1/2 c. Fortified Whey powder
1/2 c. water
Salt to taste

1. Place peas, water, celery, carrots, onions, thyme, marjoram, garlic, cayenne and bacon-flavored bits in a large kettle.
2. Bring to a boil and simmer until peas are tender and falling apart. Add water if necessary.
3. Remove from heat and pour half the soup into your blender and blend until smooth. Pour into a clean pan and repeat process with remaining soup.
4. Pour 1/2 c. hot water into blender and add 1/2 c. Fortified Whey powder. Blend until smooth and add to the pea soup. Add more water, if desired.
5. Add salt, about 1-1/2 tsp., heat and serve.

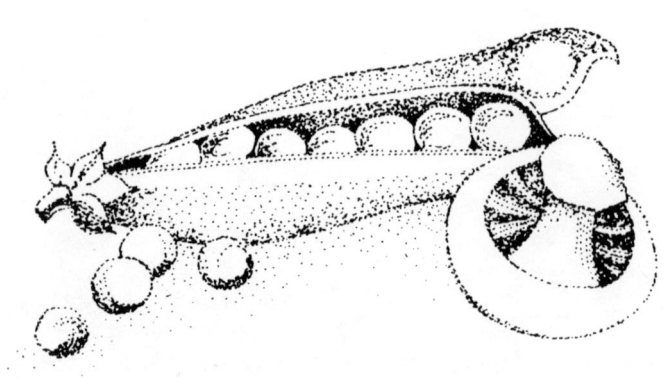

CHEDDAR CHEESE SOUP

A delicious and relatively quick soup for the family and guests.

1 med. onion, quartered
1 carrot, peeled and quartered
2-1/4 c. water
2 cans potato soup
1/3 c. Fortified Whey powder
1 Tbsp. margarine
6 oz. grated cheddar cheese

1. Put first four ingredients in blender and "grate" until smooth. Pour into kettle and simmer 10 minutes.
2. Remove from heat: add remaining ingredients, stir well, and serve when cheese is melted.
   (Garnish with croutons)

 AUNT CHRIS' POTATO SOUP

Perfect for chilly wintry lunch hours. No more cooking than boiling the potatoes.

2 lg. potatoes, diced
2 tsp. minced onion
2-1/2 c. cold water (enough to cover potatoes)
1/2 c. Fortified Whey powder
1-2 Tbsp. butter or margarine (to taste)
Dash of pepper
Dash of garlic salt
Dash of parsley

Optional: 1/4 tsp. chives
         2 Tbsp. sour cream
Parmesan cheese

1. Boil potatoes and onions in water until tender. Turn off heat.
2. Add Fortified Whey powder and stir until dissolved.
3. Add remaining ingredients and sprinkle with parmesan cheese. Serve hot.

"UNCANNY" TOMATO SOUP

Just right for warming hearts on a chilly day.

1-26 oz. can whole tomatoes, undrained, or 2-15 oz. cans stewed tomatoes
1/2 small onion, cut in chunks
1 stalk celery, cut in chunks
4 c. water
1 c. Fortified Whey powder
3 Tbsp. unbleached flour
2 tsp. honey (optional)
1 tsp. salt
1/2 tsp. pepper
1/4 tsp. crushed basil

1. Place first three ingredients in blender and "chop" for five seconds. If using stewed tomatoes, reserve one can for step 4.
2. Pour into large pan and simmer five minutes.
3. Put remaining ingredients into blender and "stir" until smooth.
4. Add to heated tomatoes, slightly cut up.
5. Bring soup to a simmer for five more minutes and serve.

For Your Recipe

AVOCADO SOUP

2 Tbsp. margarine
1/3 c. chopped green pepper
1/4 c. chopped green onion
3 chicken bouillon cubes
4 c. warm water
3 med. avocados, peeled and seeded
1/3 c. Fortified Whey powder
Dash of garlic salt, pepper

1. Sauté green pepper and onion in margarine until tender.
2. Add water and bouillon cubes. Stir to dissolve.
3. Pour over avocados and Fortified Whey in blender. Blend until smooth.
4. Add remaining seasonings, stir, and serve.

BROCCOLI SOUPREME

Make enough for Thirds!

1 pkg. (10 oz.) frozen chopped broccoli
3 c. water
3 tsp. chicken bouillon granules
1/2 c. Fortified Whey powder
1 slice mild cheddar cheese

1. Cook broccoli in water until tender. When slightly cooled, pour into blender and add remaining ingredients. Serve hot or cold, garnished with cheese croutons.

A cheerful heart has a continual feast.
Proverbs 15:15

MAIN DISHES

MAIN DISHES

The taste and textures of main dishes that call for milk are slightly, but pleasantly, changed with the substitution of Fortified Whey. If you substitute Fortified Whey for whole milk, your finished product will be slightly sweeter because of the unique carbohydrate formula of Fortified Whey, but actually lower in calories.

In this section we have included recipes that are relatively inexpensive, but very taste tempting. Most take only a few minutes of your time to prepare, but are nice enough to please your favorite guests.

The poultry and fish recipes printed here are offered as good-tasting, economical alternatives to high-cholesterol beef.

SUPER SPINACH QUICHE

Fortified Whey goes to Monte Carlo!

1 c. U-Name-It-Mix (p. 47)
1/4 c. water
2 eggs
1/4 c. chopped onion
1 bunch fresh spinach leaves, washed, chopped and stems removed
1/2 c. parmesan cheese
4 oz. grated Jack cheese
1 carton creamed cottage cheese
1/2 tsp. salt
1/4 tsp. garlic powder
2 more eggs

1. Combine mix, water, 2 eggs and onion. Beat 20 strokes. Spread in 13 x 9 x 2 greased baking pan.
2. Mix remaining ingredients and spoon evenly over batter in pan.
3. Bake at 375° for 30 minutes or until set. Let stand 5 minutes, then serve.

SUNDAY CHICKEN CASSEROLE

4 Tbsp. margarine
1 onion, chopped
1/2 c. celery, chopped
1 can (4 oz.) mushrooms, stems and pieces
1 can cream of celery soup
1 c. sour cream
2-3 c. cooked chicken, diced
1/4 tsp. salt
1/2 tsp. sage
1/8 tsp. pepper
2 c. U-Name-It-Mix (p. 47) or biscuit mix
1/3 c. Fortified Whey powder
2 eggs
1/2 c. liquid Fortified Whey
1/2 c. Shredded Jack cheese

1. Sauté onion, celery, (fresh mushrooms, if used) in margarine.
2. Add soup, sour cream, chicken, salt, pepper and sage. Simmer.
3. Spread in greased 2 qt. casserole.
4. Mix together eggs, biscuit mix, powder, liquid and cheese, stirring only until moistened.
5. Spoon over chicken mixture.
6. Bake at 350° until golden brown on top, about 30 minutes.

Serves 6-8

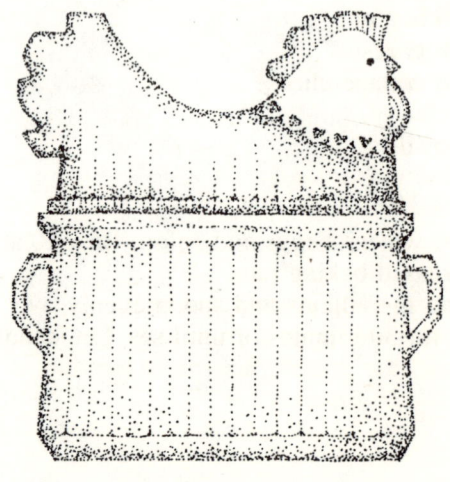

DAD'S FAVORITE BAKED CHICKEN

This recipe is aromatic, easy to put together and bakes without bother in the oven.

2-1/2 - 3 lb. chicken, cut up and skinned
1 onion, sliced
1 Tbsp. chopped parsley
1/4 c. sliced celery
1/2 c. sliced mushrooms
1/2 tsp. rosemary
1/4 tsp. thyme
1/2 tsp. salt
Pepper
2 c. white sauce (p. 23)
1/3 c. white wine

1. Place chicken in casserole with lid.
2. Sprinkle the next 8 ingredients over chicken.
3. Top with white sauce and white wine. (p. 23)
4. Cover and bake at 450° for 50 minutes.
5. Serve with rice or Fortified Whey whipped potatoes.

TUNA CASSEROLE -ITALIAN STYLE

6 oz. egg noodles
1 can cream of mushroom soup
1/2 c. Fortified Whey liquid
1 c. Yofresh or yogurt
1/2 c. chopped green onion
1/3 c. parmesan cheese
1 can (6 oz.) tuna in water
1 can (4 oz.) sliced mushrooms
1/2 c. spanish olives, sliced

1. Partially cook noodles and set aside.
2. Combine remaining ingredients and heat.
3. Mix with noodles and pour into greased 1-1/2 quart casserole.
4. Sprinkle with a little grated cheese and paprika.
5. Bake at 375° for 20 minutes.

CHILI RELLENO CASSEROLE

Serve this with Spanish rice and an avocado salad.

1 can diced chilies - 4 oz.
3/4 lb. shredded Jack cheese
1 c. U-Name-It-Mix (p. 47) or biscuit mix
6 eggs
3 c. water
1/2 c. Fortified Whey rounded
2 tsp. paprika
1/2 tsp. salt
1/2 tsp. oregano
1/4 tsp. each pepper, garlic powder, dry mustard

1. Butter bottom and sides of 10" x 10" casserole dish.
2. Sprinkle chilies, then cheese in bottom.
3. In separate bowl, combine all dry ingredients and mix thoroughly.
4. Add eggs and water to dry mixture and beat with wire whisk or electric mixer for 1 minute.
5. Pour over cheese and chilies.
6. Bake at 350° for 50-55 minutes, until high and golden brown.
7. Serve as is or with a tomato salsa.

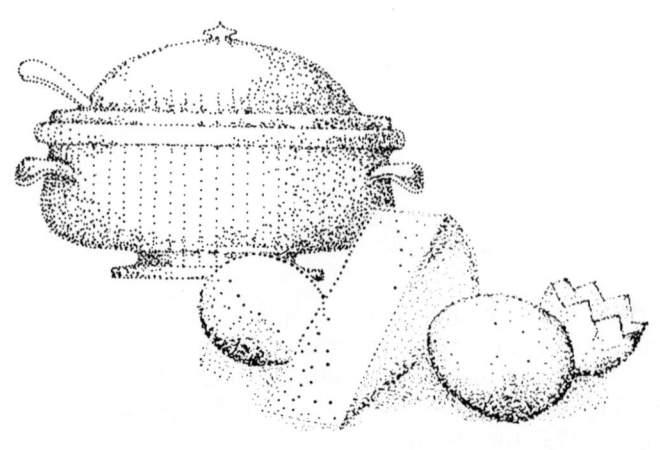

SAVORY BAKED SNAPPER

Fish has an important part to play in a well balanced diet. Fortified Whey offers a way of preparing it that makes it extra nourishing.

1 lb. red snapper fillets (cod and sole can also be used)
1 c. white sauce (p. 23)
1 Tbsp. vinegar
1/2 tsp. each salt, oregano, basil, and onion powder
1 c. shredded Gruyere cheese
1/3 c. grated Romano cheese

1. Lay fillets in buttered 8" baking dish. If using frozen fillets, cut partially thawed block into four pieces.
2. Mix remaining ingredients in separate bowl and stir until well blended.
3. Pour evenly over fish.
4. Cover and bake 30 minutes at 400°, and serve garnished with a sprig of fresh parsley.

Helpful Hint: When making luscious mashed potatoes, drain boiled potatoes. Add seasonings, 2 Tbsp. butter or margarine and 1/4 c. Fortified Whey powder to 2 c. potatoes and mix well. Add water only if needed.

Helpful Hint: In our experiments with meatloaf and meatballs, we found that adding 1/4 c. Fortified Whey powder to 2 c. meat mixture improves the texture and consistency of the finished dish and brings out the flavor of the meat. You are sure to like this if you like meatloaf sandwiches or Swedish or Italian meatballs

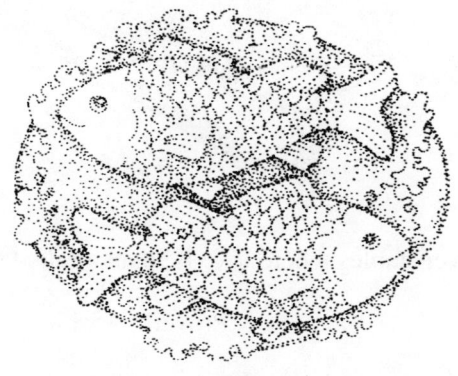

MUSHROOM AND ARTICHOKE CASSEROLE

Truly an outstanding vegetable dish.

3 c. fresh mushrooms, halved
1/2 c. sliced green onions with tops
1/4 c. butter
2 Tbsp. unbleached flour
1 c. water
1 tsp. instant chicken bouillon granules
1 tsp. lemon juice
1/8 tsp. nutmeg
2 Tbsp. Fortified Whey
10 oz. pkg. frozen artichoke hearts, cooked & drained
3/4 c. soft whole wheat bread crumbs (1 slice)
1 Tbsp. melted butter

1. Cook mushrooms and green onions in butter until slightly melted.
2. Remove vegetables from pan, leaving juices.
3. Blend flour, 1/8 tsp. salt, and a dash of pepper into pan juices.
4. Add water, bouillon, lemon juice, and nutmeg, Fortified Whey. Stir with whisk.
5. Cook and stir until bubbly.
6. Add mushrooms, onion, and artichoke hearts, and stir.
7. Pour into greased 1 qt. casserole and top with bread crumbs and melted butter, sprinkled around the edge of dish.
8. Bake at 350° for 20 minutes.

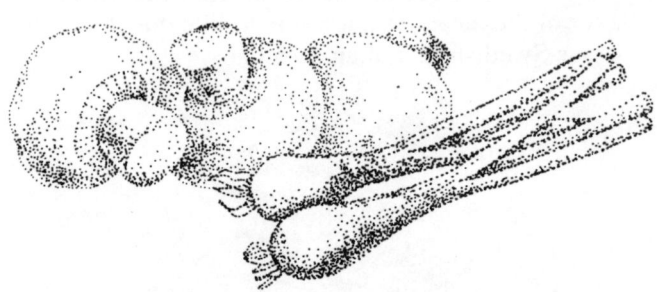

Better is a dish of vegetables where love is, than a fatted ox and hatred with it.

Proverbs 15:17

SAUCES AND GRAVIES

SAUCES AND GRAVIES

Fortified Whey liquid can be substituted equally for milk in most sauces and gravies. The unique thing about the powder is that it can be dissolved directly into hot stock or meat drippings and water added if necessary.

NEVER-FAIL CHICKEN OR BEEF GRAVY

So tasty for being so quick.

1/4 c. Fortified Whey powder
2 c. hot tap water
1 bouillon cube - chicken or beef
1/4 c. diced green or white onion
2 Tbsp. flour
Dash garlic salt
Dash pepper

1. Dissolve bouillon cube and Fortified Whey in hot water.
2. Sauté onions and garlic salt and pepper in butter.
3. Sprinkle on flour and stir.
4. Turn off heat.
5. Add bouillon broth and stir until ingredients are blended together.
6. Heat and stir until thickened.

Variations: You can add your own variation to this basic gravy such as including diced green pepper or mushrooms with the sauteed onions when choosing the beef bouillon. The chicken gravy can be turned into a fantastic sauce for fettucine. Make the basic chicken gravy. Add 1 Tbsp. chives, 1/2 c. sour cream, 1/2 can cream of mushroom soup. Melt in 2 medium slices of Jack cheese. Pour over chicken and fettucine and you will be surprised — what a meal with your favorite steamed vegetable.

CREAMY WHITE SAUCE

Double this recipe and store in refrigerator for the many easy sauces you will make.

1/4 c. margarine
1/4 c. flour
1/3 c. Fortified Whey powder
2 c. water
Salt to taste

1. In saucepan, melt margarine and sprinkle in flour, stirring to keep smooth.
2. Slowly add 1 c. water, a little at a time. Then remaining water.
3. Bring to a boil and simmer 1 minute. Remove from heat, stir in Fortified Whey powder with wire whisk.
4. Serve and season as desired.

Helpful Hint: For a cheese sauce, add 3/4 tsp. mustard, 1/2 tsp. vinegar, (1/4 tsp. onion powder optional) 1 c. grated cheddar cheese and 1/2 c. more Fortified Whey. Serve over vegetables or fish.

For a curry sauce, add 1 tsp. curry powder.

For Your Recipe

DESSERTS

DESSERTS

In this book we have a rather large offering of dessert recipes. The majority of our recipes here attempt to cut down on the amount of sweetener normally associated with each dessert, and try to use whole grains wherever possible. Hopefully we can help to minimize the number of empty calories we usually have in desserts.

Fortified Whey is so versatile in both powdered and liquid forms, you will find many opportunities to add essential nutrients to your family's diet with the addition of this wonderful new ingredient.

RICH'S APPLESAUCE CAROB CAKE

2-1/4 c. Soft-as-a-Cloud Carob Cake Mix (p. 47)
1/3 c. safflower oil
1 c. unsweetened applesauce
1 egg
3/4 c. honey

1. Place mix, oil, egg and applesauce in a bowl.
2. Beat well by hand or with electric mixer for two minutes.
3. Pour into greased 8" or 9" square pan.
4. Bake 35-40 minutes at 350°.
5. Cool cake and frost if desired with a thin cream cheese frosting.

This cake has a beautiful texture and stays soft and moist.

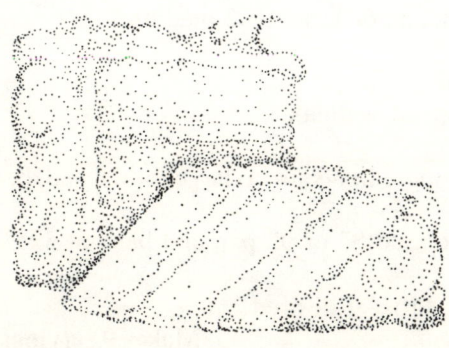

"NUTS-ABOUT-CAROB" CAKE

3/4 c. honey
2-1/4 c. Soft-as-a-Cloud Carob Cake Mix (p. 47)
1 egg
1/3 c. safflower oil
1 c. Yofresh
1/2 tsp. vanilla
1/2 c. carob chips
1/2 c. chopped nuts

1. Combine first six ingredients and beat well with electric mixer, or by hand, for two minutes.
2. Pour into greased 8" or 9" pan.
3. Sprinkle carob chips and nuts over the top.
4. Bake at 350° for 35-40 minutes.

This cake is so soft, it is hard to cut until almost entirely cool. If you can't wait (like the rest of us) make two cakes and have it both ways! It's great!

BANANA SPICE CAKE

Even better the second day!

2-1/4 c. Beautifully Basic Cake Mix (p. 48)
1/3 c. oil
1/2 c. honey
1 egg
1/2 c. liquid Fortified Whey
1 tsp. lemon juice
1/2 c. mashed banana (1 large or 2 medium)
3/4 tsp. nutmeg
3/4 tsp. cinnamon
1/2 c. finely chopped walnuts

1. Combine all ingredients in a large bowl and beat well for 2-3 minutes.
2. Pour into a greased 8" or 9" pan and bake at 325° for 30-35 minutes.
3. Cool on rack. Frost if desired.

                    Makes 9 servings.

COCONUT PINEAPPLE SNACK CAKE

It's not too sweet!

2-1/4 c. Beautifully Basic Cake Mix (p. 48)
3/4 c. crushed unsweetened pineapple - undrained
1/4 c. Yofresh or yogurt
1 egg
1/4 c. oil
1/4 c. water
1/2 c. honey
1 tsp. vanilla

1. Combine cake ingredients and beat well - about 3 minutes.
2. Pour into greased 9" square pan.
3. Bake 325° for about 40-45 minutes.
4. While cake is baking, make coconut topping.
5. When cake is done, remove from oven and spread with topping and return to oven until coconut is toasted.

Toasted Coconut Topping

1/4 c. honey
1 c. shredded coconut
3 Tbsp. butter
2 Tbsp. Fortified Whey

1. Cream butter and honey.
2. Add Fortified Whey and mix again.
3. Add coconut and stir.
4. Spread on hot cake and return to oven for about 5 minutes or broil 4-5 inches from heat.
5. Remove from oven and serve warm.

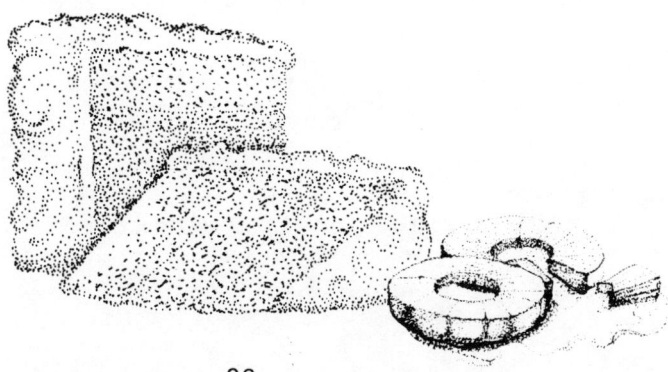

POPPY SEED POUND CAKE

Deliciously Different.

2/3 c. margarine
3/4 c. honey
6 eggs
3 c. unbleached flour (can use half whole wheat flour)
1/3 c. powdered Fortified Whey
1/4 tsp. baking soda
1/2 tsp. salt
3/4 c. Yofresh
2 tsp. vanilla
1/3 c. poppy seeds

1. Cream butter and honey until light and fluffy.
2. Add eggs, one at a time, beat well after each addition.
3. Combine flour, powdered Fortified Whey, soda and salt.
4. Add alternately, with Yofresh or yogurt, to creamed mixture.
5. Stir in vanilla and poppy seeds.
6. Pour into greased and floured 10" tube pan.
7. Bake at 325° for 1 hour and 30 minutes or until tested done.
8. Cool in pan 10 minutes. Remove from pan and cool on rack.
9. Store covered in refrigerator for two days for best flavor.

Delicious when served with fresh fruit or ice cream.

AUTUMN EVENING DOUGHNUTS

This is an easy, old-fashioned favorite.

2 c. unbleached flour
3 tsp. baking powder
2 Tbsp. honey
1/4 c. Fortified Whey powder
1/4 tsp. salt
1/4 tsp. nutmeg
1 egg
1/4 c. vegetable oil
1/2 c. water
1/2 tsp. vanilla
Cooking oil for frying (deep enough to float doughnut)

1. Combine first six ingredients in bowl.
2. Blend next for ingredients in separate bowl. Then add to dry ingredients.
3. Stir until well blended and knead lightly 3-5 minutes.
4. Drop by teaspoonfuls into hot oil and fry for about 3 minutes until nut brown.
5. Drain on paper towels.
6. Sprinkle with cinnamon or date sugar.

Eat warm with hot cider or an herb tea.

COCONUT MERINGUE COOKIES

This cookie is made without flour!

4 egg whites
2 Tbsp. honey
1 tsp. almond extract
4 Tbsp. powdered Fortified Whey
1 c. flaked coconut

1. Beat egg whites until stiff.
2. Drizzle in honey and continue beating.
3. Fold in almond extract, Fortified Whey and coconut.
4. Spoon onto greased cookie sheet and bake at 275° for 20 minutes.
5. Cool slightly before removing.

This little cookie is tricky to get off the pan, but worth the effort and best when cool.

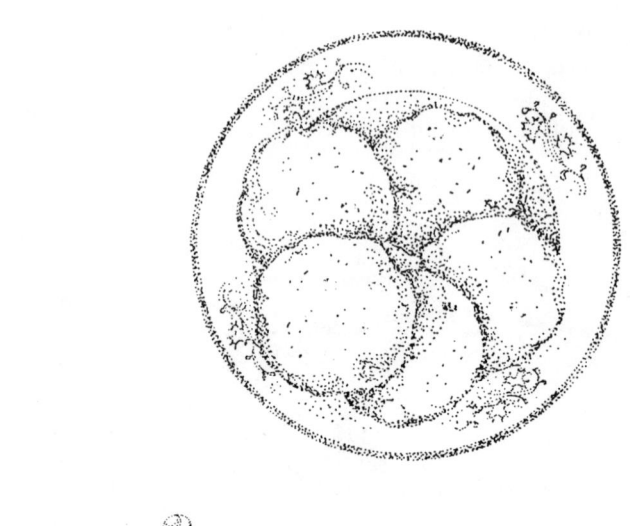

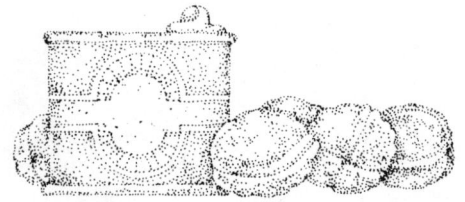

PUMPKIN COOKIES

A great alternate to holiday pumpkin pie!

1/2 c. honey
1/2 c. shortening
2/3 c. water
2 eggs
1-3/4 c. canned pumpkin
1/2 c. Fortified Whey powder
2-3/4 c. unbleached flour
1 Tbsp. baking powder
1 tsp. cinnamon
1/2 tsp. nutmeg
1/2 tsp. salt
1/4 tsp. ginger
1 c. raisins
1 c. chopped pecans

1. Heat oven to 400°. Mix honey, shortening, eggs and pumpkin thoroughly.
2. Measure flour and blend dry ingredients.
3. Add to pumpkin mixture with water, stirring until well blended.
4. Add raisins and pecans.
5. Drop batter by teaspoonfuls on ungreased baking sheet.
6. Bake 12-15 minutes or until lightly brown.
7. Cookies may be iced when cool with a thin butter icing.

Makes 6 dozen

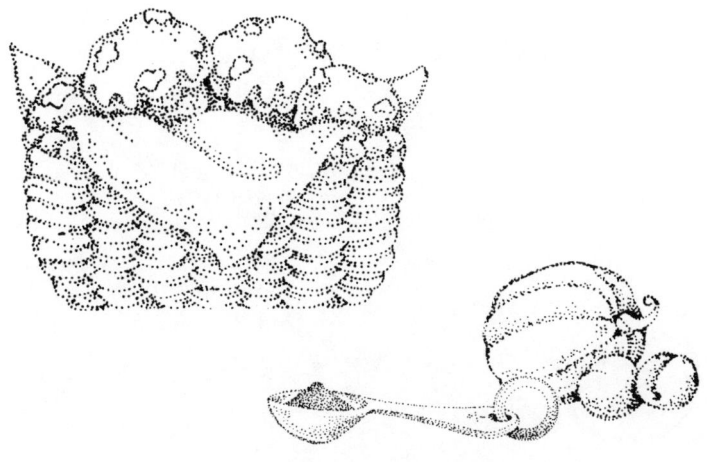

FRUIT GEM COOKIES

Children love them!

1 egg
1/3 c. oil
1/4 c. honey
2 Tbsp. Fortified Whey powder
1/2 tsp. soda
2 Tbsp. Yofresh or yogurt
1/2 tsp. vanilla
Dash of salt
1 c. whole wheat or unbleached flour
Raspberry or apple preserves, or preserves of your choice.

1. Beat first six ingredients together, then add and blend the remaining ingredients, except preserves.
2. Chill well.
3. Drop by teaspoonful onto greased cookie sheet and make an indentation with your thumb in the center of each cookie.
4. Fill each hole with preserves.
5. Bake at 350° for 10-12 minutes.

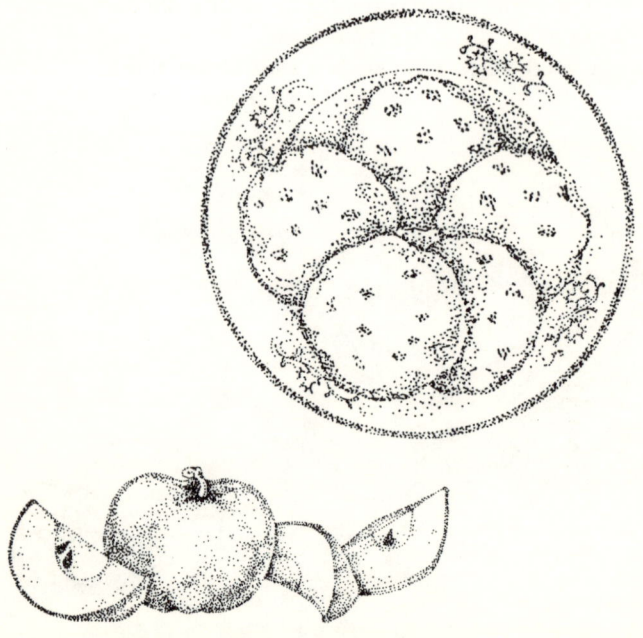

PEANUT-GRANOLA DROPS

A great energy pick-er-up-er.

3/4 c. granola
1/2 c. natural peanut butter
1/2 c. Fortified Whey powder
1/2 c. honey
1/4 c. sesame seeds, chopped dates or raisins

Coating: granola, flaked coconut, sesame seeds, or crushed bran cereal

1. Mix all ingredients, working with fingers, if necessary.
2. Shape into small cherry-size balls or little logs.
3. Roll in your choice of coating and place in single layer in container with cover and refrigerate.

                              Makes 3 dozen

For Your Recipe

BANANA FRESH PIE

Without artificial flavoring

1. Make one recipe of Basic Vanilla Pudding (p. 49)
2. After the pudding is done and still in the pan, add 2 medium sliced bananas that have been coated with lemon juice and 1 c. cold water, drain and discard lemon water—Pour into pre-baked pie shell and chill.

Optional: Top with whipped Yofresh topper (p. 3)

Helpful Hint: When using your favorite pumpkin pie recipe, substitute 1/3 c. Fortified Whey powder (dissolved in water-1-1/2 c.) for every 1-1/2 c. cream called for in the recipe.

GRANDMA'S BREAD PUDDING

An old-time favorite

1 c. dry bread cubes
1-1/2 c. water
1/4 c. Fortified Whey powder rounded
1/4 c. honey
1/2 tsp. cinnamon
1 tsp. vanilla
2 eggs, beaten lightly
3 Tbsp. raisins

1. Set oven temp. at 325°.
2. Soak bread cubes in water mixed with powder for 5 minutes.
3. Stir in honey, cinnamon, raisins and eggs.
4. Add vanilla and mix evenly.
5. Bake in a greased baking dish for about 45-55 minutes or until firm.

CAROB PUDDING

Smooth and rich.

2-1/2 c. cold Fortified Whey liquid
4 Tbsp. cornstarch
1/3 c. honey
1/2 tsp. vanilla
1/4 c. carob powder

1. Mix 1/2 c. of cold Fortified Whey with the cornstarch, honey and vanilla. Blend until smooth.
2. Slowly blend the carob powder into the honey mixture.
3. Heat the remaining 2 c. of Fortified Whey in a saucepan. Add the carob mixture, stirring briskly and cook, stirring constantly until it thickens.
4. Cool before serving.

FROZEN VANILLA DESSERT

Get out your ice cream maker!

3/4 c. clover honey
2 c. non-dairy whipped topping or non-dairy cream
2 egg yolks
2 Tbsp. vanilla extract
2 c. Fortified Whey powder
7 c. water

1. Blend all ingredients with electric mixer or blender. Pour into freezing can of ice cream freezer.
2. Follow directions for making ice cream from the manufacturer's guide that comes with your ice cream freezer. It takes about 50-60 minutes to freeze to soft ice cream consistancy.
3. For freezer tray method, see p. 39.

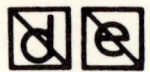 **WILD BLACKBERRY FROZEN DESSERT**

An outstanding dessert for a special occasion.

1 lb. pkg. frozen blackberries
2/3 c. clover honey
1 c. water
4 Tbsp. lemon juice
3/4 c. Fortified Whey powder, 2-1/2 c. water
1 c. cream or non-dairy creamer-optional

1. Empty frozen blackberries into blender.
2. Warm honey and water in saucepan until honey is dissolved. Pour over blackberries in blender and "blend."
3. Empty blackberry puree into bowl and add remaining ingredients (blend Fortified Whey with cream in blender, then add to puree).
4. Process like ice cream in ice cream freezer 50-60 minutes.

 HONEY & CAROB ICE DREAM

1-1/2 c. Fortified Whey powder
1 c. carob sauce
1/2 c. honey
1 Tbsp. vanilla
6 c. water
2 c. non-dairy whipping cream or 2 c. cream whipped

1. Make sauce & cool to lukewarm. Add honey & dissolve. Mix Fortified Whey with part of the water in blender. Pour in can. Stir in honey & carob mixture. Mix cream, remaining water and vanilla in blender & add to can. Process like ice cream.

Carob Sauce

1 c. carob powder (unsweetened)
1 c. water

1. Heat in saucepan, low heat, stirring constantly. Cook 5-8 minutes until smooth. Cool and store in refrigerator. Add 1/4 c. honey and 2 Tbsp. butter while mixture is warm if desire to sweeten.

SUMMER PEACH FREEZE

Simply the best you've ever tasted!

4 c. peach puree (5 c. fresh peach slices or peaches in juice, drained)
1 c. Fortified Whey powder
3-1/2 c. water
2/3 c. clover or orange honey
1 Tbsp. unsulphured molasses
2 tsp. lemon juice
1 c. whipped topping (non-dairy)

Combine all ingredients and process like ice cream in an ice cream freezer. It takes 50-60 minutes to complete the freezing.

NO-CHEESE-CHEESE CAKE

1 envelope unflavored gelatine
1-1/4 c. Vanilla Pudding Mix (p. 49)
2-1/2 Tbsp. honey
5 Tbsp. lemon juice
1/2 c. whipped cream

1. Place first three ingredients in a saucepan and stir. Allow to sit one minute.
2. Cook over medium heat stirring constantly until mixture comes to a boil. Remove from heat and add honey.
3. Pour into a large bowl and chill, stirring on and off until mixture mounds slightly when dropped from a spoon.
4. Stir in lemon juice and whipped cream.
5. Pour into prepared 9" pie crust. (prefer graham cracker).
6. Chill until firm.
7. Before serving, top with fresh or frozen cherries, thawed.

FABULOUS FRUIT FREEZE

Double this to fit in ice cream maker. Fantastic!

1 qt. Yofresh
1/3 c. honey (clover, preferred)
1 c. fresh or frozen fruit of your choice (strawberries, peaches, blueberries, etc.)

1. Spoon Yofresh into cream can of ice cream freezer.
2. Process fruit in blender at highest speed and add honey.
3. Pour fruit mixture over Fortified Whey in can.
4. Process according to manufacturers directions until Freeze is thick. Eat immediately or store in plastic container in freezer.

FROZEN YOFRESH BARS

Gives empty calorie treats real competition.

2 c. any flavor Yofresh
1/4 c. Fortified Whey powder
1/2 tsp. honey (to taste)

1. Place Yofresh in freezer until firm, but not frozen solid.
2. Take out and place in blender with honey and Fortified Whey powder and blend until creamy in texture.
3. Pour into 6 plastic popsicle freezer containers.
4. Place in freezer until firm.
5. Serve as a frozen bar treat.

THE FRUIT BAR

The one you've always wondered how they make.

1. Use your favorite fruit juice.
2. Add 1/3 c. Fortified Whey powder to 2 c. juice.
3. Heat to just before boiling.
4. Allow to cool before placing in plastic popsicle containers.
5. Freeze and serve as a frozen bar.

Kids will love it and moms will love the "no sugar."

MINT CAROB CHIP ICE-DREAM

3 c. fortified whey powder
9 c. water
¾ c. honey
3 eggs well beaten
2 tsp. mint extract
2 tsp. vanilla extract
2½ c. non-dairy whipped topping
1 c. carob chips

1. Mix everything but chips in any order desired, to get a smooth liquid. Chill well.
2. Pour into ice cream freezer and process until soft frozen.
3. Open freezer can, add chips, then continue to freeze until machine stops. Serve immediately or let harden overnight for a firmer texture.

"MORE, PLEASE" STRAWBERRY FREEZE

You can make this one in your freezing compartment.

1 lb. frozen unsweetened strawberries or
1 qt. fresh strawberries
1/2 c. honey
3-1/2 c. water, divided
3/4 c. Fortified Whey powder
1 Tbsp. vanilla
2 Tbsp. lemon juice
2 egg yolks
1 c. non-dairy whipped topping (optional)

1. Empty frozen berries into blender.
2. Warm honey and 1 c. water in a saucepan. Pour over strawberries in blender and "blend."
3. Empty strawberry puree into large bowl.
4. Combine all remaining ingredients in blender and process until smooth. Add to strawberry puree in bowl.
5. Mix well and pour dessert into freezer trays.
6. Place trays in freezer until dessert is partially frozen.
7. Remove from trays and beat until smooth but not melted, and then return to trays and freeze until firm.
8. You can also make this in your ice cream freezer.

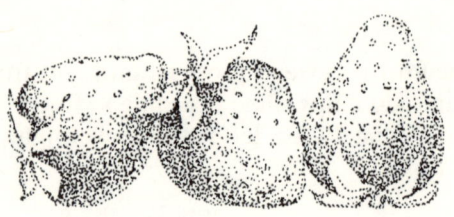

Pleasant words are like a honeycomb, sweetness to the soul and health to the body.

Proverbs 16:24

BREAD

BREAD

Fortified Whey powder does very nice things to breads. You will notice a smoother texture and, when cooking with unbleached flour, an end-product that often rises higher! And if you freeze your breads, they seem to be more moist when thawed and tasted.

Since we cannot include a recipe for everyone's favorite bread, we have only printed some relatively quick and easy breads. But may we suggest you try adding Fortified Whey powder to **your** favorite bread recipe? You **will** see a delightful difference!

QUICK BREADS USING THE U-NAME-IT-MIX

Here are the basics!
(p. 47)

	Mix	Water
Oven: 425"		
Dumplings or Drop Biscuits (10-12 min)	3 c.	3/4 c.
Rolled Biscuits (10-12 min)	3 c.	2/3 c.
Pancakes and Waffles	2-1/4 c.	1-1/2 c.
Plus 1 Tbsp. honey, 1 egg		

Helpful Hint: Susan's method - cook dumplings with lid on for 30-40 minutes. They will be lighter than air and melt in your mouth.

Helpful Hint: Chris' method - add 1 tsp. chives. Put about 1 Tbsp. mixture in large spoon. Hold down to bottom of pan of simmering to boiling liquid until dumpling pops up (will have a puffed up appearance). Follow procedure for each dumpling until all the mixture is used. Allow to simmer uncovered until the dumplings are flaky on the inside when tested - about 20-30 minutes.

EASY FRENCH BREAD

This bread is soft and fragrant.

2 pkg. yeast
1/2 c. warm water (110°)
3 Tbsp. honey
6 c. unbleached flour
3/4 c. Fortified Whey powder
1 Tbsp. salt
2 c. warm water
2 Tbsp. oil

1. Dissolve yeast in warm water in 1 qt. bowl and add honey. Set aside to bubble.
2. Combine all dry ingredients in large bowl. Mix well.
3. Add remaining water and oil to yeast mixture and pour into dry ingredients. Mix until smooth, adding 1/2 c. more flour to reach kneading consistency.
4. Knead 3 minutes.
5. Divide dough in half. Form 2 loaves and place on greased cookie sheet. Cut 3 diagonal slashes across the top and let rise.
6. Bake at 450° for 25 minutes.
7. Remove from pans to cool.

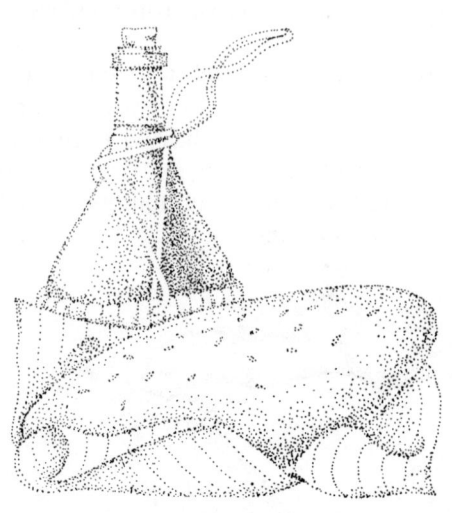

QUICK IRISH SODA BREAD

Looks great on your table.

2 c. unbleached or whole wheat flour
1-1/2 tsp. baking powder
1/4 tsp. baking soda
1/2 tsp. salt
1/3 c. Fortified Whey powder
2 Tbsp. honey
1/2 c. raisins and/or nuts
1 c. Fortified Whey liquid, soured with 1 Tbsp. vinegar

1. Sift together first 6 ingredients.
2. Add raisins and nuts.
3. Stir in soured Fortified Whey and honey.
4. Knead dough for 1 minute.
5. Shape dough into round loaf and place in greased 8" round pan.
6. Dust top with flour and cut a deep "X" into the top.
7. Bake 40 minutes at 350°.

Helpful Hint: For a nice taste twist, add 1 Tbsp. caraway seeds to dry ingredients.

Helpful Hint: To add Fortified Whey powder to your favorite bread, simply follow this rule of thumb: 1/4 c. Fortified Whey powder, added to dry ingredients, for every 2 to 3 c. flour. That's it!

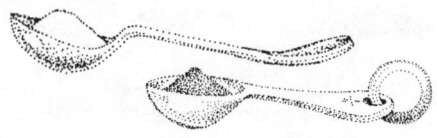

SUSAN'S SUNRISE MUFFINS

Golden brown and rich with raisins.

2 c. whole wheat flour
1/2 c. powdered Fortified Whey
1/4 c. honey
1 tsp. baking soda
1/2 tsp. salt
1 c. raisins
1 c. hot water
1/4 c. safflower oil
1 tsp. vanilla

1. Heat oven to 350°. Grease 12 c. muffin (cupcake) tin.
2. Combine all dry ingredients with raisins.
3. Stir in liquids until all particles are moistened.
4. Spoon into cupcake tin.
5. Bake 20-25 minutes.

Helpful Hint: These muffins can be frozen and warmed later to delight your overnight guests.

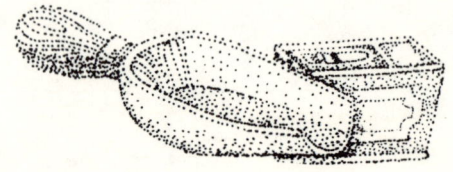

YEAST FINGER BREAD - NO RISING!

Good to make ahead.

All ingredients at room temperature.

2 cakes or 2 pkgs. dry yeast
2/3 c. water
1/2 c. margarine
2 egg yolks
1/3 c. honey
1/2 c. sour cream
3 c. unbleached flour
1/3 c. Fortified Whey powder
1/3 c. chopped nuts
1 tsp. cinnamon
1/4 tsp. nutmeg

1. Dissolve yeast in warm water.
2. Cream margarine and honey.
3. Add egg yolks and mix.
4. Add sour cream with yeast.
5. Add to margarine and honey mixture.
6. Gradually sift flour, spices and Fortified Whey powder into first mixture.
7. Chill dough 2-3 hours or overnight.
8. Remove from refrigerator.
9. Break off walnut-size pieces of dough and roll between palms to the size of your largest finger. Twist two together like a braid. Lay on greased cookie sheet.
10. Bake at 325° for 20-25 minutes.

Twists are great for treats and not too sweet.

For Your Recipe

Better is a dry morsel and quietness with it, than a house full of feasting with strife.

Proverbs 17:1

BASIC MIXES

BASIC MIXES

Fortified Whey responds well in so many areas of baking that we decided to make basic mixes in larger quantities and use these mixes instead of buying packaged mixes of inferior quality at the grocery store.

The first mix we tried was a pudding mix, and it was so delicious and so amazingly simple, that we knew every Fortified Whey lover would want to have a jar or two of it in their pantry.

For maximum freshness, store your mixes in airtight jars or freezer storage bags. Then, attach a sticker labeling the mix and recording the date packaged.

Helpful Hint: Knowing that Fortified Whey powder needs to be stored in a cool, dark place, if the mix is placed in a clear glass or plastic canister it needs to be stored in a cupboard rather than on the countertop. Solid metal or similar containers can be a countertop item.

An attractive label can name the mix with a matching label on the back of the canister to give mixing instructions.

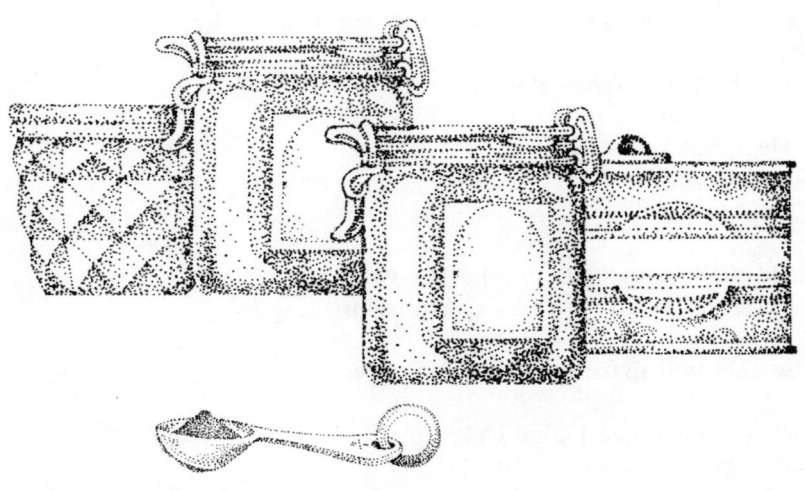

QUICK BREADS USING THE U-NAME-IT-MIX

Biscuits, Pancakes, Waffles, Dumplings (p. 40)

8-1/2 c. unbleached flour
1 Tbsp. baking powder
1 Tbsp. salt
2 tsp. cream of tarter
1 tsp. baking soda
1-1/4 c. Fortified Whey powder
1-3/4 c. vegetable shortening

1. Sift dry ingredients. Blend well.
2. Cut in shortening until evenly distributed.
3. Put in large airtight container.
4. Label.
5. Store in cool, dry place.
6. Use within 10-12 weeks. Makes about 13 c. of mix.

Variation: Use 4-1/4 c. unbleached flour and 4-1/4 c. whole wheat flour instead of 8-1/2 c. white flour. Increase baking powder to 2 Tbsp.

SOFT-AS-A-CLOUD-CAROB CAKE MIX

You'll use this a lot, so better make a double batch.

4 c. unbleached flour (Whole wheat can be used. Leave out 1/4 c. flour)
1/2 c. Fortified Whey Powder
1-1/2 tsp. baking soda
2 Tbsp. baking powder
1-1/2 tsp. salt
1/2 c. carob

1. Mix all ingredients in a large bowl.
2. Transfer mix to container with tight-fitting lid.

This mix will make the following cakes:

Rich's Applesauce Fudge Cake (p. 24)
Nuts-About-Carob Cake (p. 25)

BEAUTIFULLY BASIC CAKE MIX

A versatile, low-sugar friend.

8 c. unbleached flour
1 c. Fortified Whey powder
1/4 c. baking powder
1 Tbsp. baking soda
1 Tbsp. salt

1. Mix all ingredients well.
2. Store and label.

This mix will make the following cakes:

Banana Spice Cake (p. 25)
Coconut Pineapple Snack Cake (p. 26)

CAROB PUDDING MIX

This pudding is lower in calories and more economical than the "store-bought" pudding mixes.

4 c. Fortified Whey White Mix
1 c. cornstarch
1/2 c. carob

1. Stir together.
2. Store in airtight container.

To make excellent fudge pudding:
1/4 c. honey
1. In saucepan stir together 1-1/4 c. pudding mix and 2-1/2 c. water.
2. Bring to a boil, stirring constantly.
3. Boil 1 minute and remove from heat.
4. Add 1/2 tsp. vanilla.
5. Pour into serving dishes and chill.

BASIC VANILLA PUDDING MIX

A velvety, light pudding.

4 c. Fortified Whey powder
1 c. cornstarch

1. Stir together.
2. Store in airtight container.

To make pudding:

1-1/4 c. pudding mix
2 Tbsp. honey
1 tsp. vanilla
2-1/2 c. water

1. In saucepan stir together 1-1/4 c. pudding mix and 2-1/2 c. water.
2. Bring to boil. stirring constantly.
3. Boil 1 minute and remove from heat. Stir in 2 Tbsp. honey.
4. Add 1 tsp. vanilla and 1 drop yellow food coloring.
5. Pour into serving dishes and chill.

Variations: Top chilled pudding with grated coconut or granola, or fold in fresh, sliced strawberries, apricots, peaches or pears. Chopped dates and nuts are another great addition.

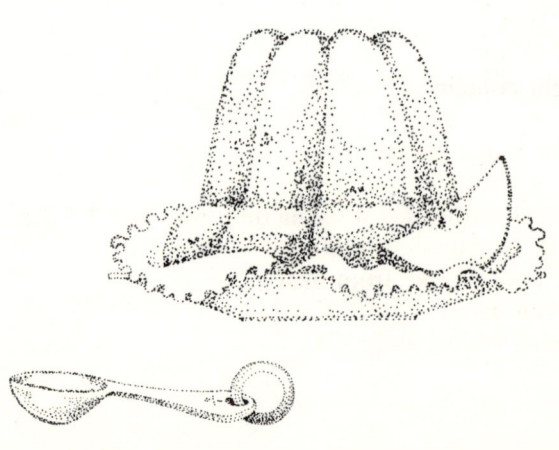

FORTIFIED WHEY MAKES A GRAND-OLA

Dry Ingredients

3 c. oatmeal
1 c. rolled wheat
1/2 c. wheat germ
1/2 c. bran
2 c. nuts and seeds
1 c. coconut
Fortified Whey powder to coat

Wet ingredients

1/4 c. honey
1/4 c. oil
1/2 c. water
Vanilla to taste

Add later: raisins, dried fruit, dates

1. Combine the dry and wet ingredients separately.
2. Then stir evenly the wet ingredients into the dry.
3. Bake in lightly oiled baking pan for 1-1/2 hours at 250° until granola is dry and lightly browned and crisp.
4. Remove from oven and add fruit.
5. Cool and store in airtight container.

For Your Recipe

 **TAKE-ALONG-BREAKFAST CEREAL**

Take this when you camp or travel. All you'll need is a bowl and cold water for a yummy breakfast!

2 c. granola, any variety
1/2 c. flaked coconut
1/4 c. raisins (1/4 c. sunflower seeds optional)
3/4 c. Fortified Whey powder

1. Mix all ingredients and store in airtight container.
2. To serve, pour desired amount into bowl or cup. Add water (hot or cold) stir and eat.

Recipe can be doubled and ingredients varied.

Helpful Hint: Try 1/4 c. chopped peanuts, sunflower seeds, dried apples or all-bran cereal with this breakfast cereal. It is so convenient and tasty!

Helpful Hint: You don't need to have your Fortified Whey mixed up to use it with your hot cereal. Add boiling water to the Take-Along-Cereal mix **or** put 3/4 c. of your favorite granola in 1 c. boiling water. When it softens, add 1/8 c. Fortified Whey. Stir and cool to taste. You will love the smooth texture.

Try nature's new "whey" to the land of health and honey. The new and original "whey" powder adds nutritional depth to your favorite recipes.

ABOUT THE AUTHOR

Joe M. Parkhill is a Professor of Apiculture. He has been awarded the degree of Honeyologist from the Board of Directors of the International Preventive Medicine Foundation for making possible increased professional and public awareness of the vital need for the practice of holistic preventive medicine, health care and the value of improved nutrient composition in natural foods and to minimize the ugly fat bulges when one overindulges.

For many years Joe has traveled far and wide to gather the material and insight necessary to become the most qualified and outspoken exponent of the value of preventive medicine. He was awarded the Golden Bee Award for his lectures on the nutritional value of honey — its use in preventive medicine, as a beauty aid, the overall health value, in short — the many reasons to use honey in everyday living.

Parkhill has produced the movie "Cooking with Honey" which he uses on many of his lecture tours and TV/Radio appearances. Topics included in his lecture are: That too tired feeling — Too run down when night comes! — Are you eating yourself to death? — Overeating is not the main reason for being overweight!

Joe M. Parkhill is the author and publisher of the most popular and fastest selling sugarless cookbook ever, **The Wonderful World of Honey**. His book, **Health — Beauty — Happiness -- How To Have It — How To Keep It**, is the only book of its kind ever to be published.

GOLDEN HONEYED CHICKEN

1 fryer [3-3½ lb.]
4 T. butter, melted
½ c. mushrooms
1 c. rich milk
½ c. honey
flour to dredge
salt and pepper

Cut chicken into serving size pieces. Season with salt and pepper (cayenne may be used). Dust with flour. Arrange in flat baking dish or roaster. Pour melted butter over top. Place in hot oven (400°), uncovered, ½ hour to brown. Then reduce heat to moderate temperature. Mix milk with honey. Pour over chicken and bake 1 hour. Add mushrooms, 15 minutes before serving. Serves 4-5.

CARROT CAKE

⅔ C. FLOUR
1½ c. honey
2 t. baking soda
2 t. cinnamon
1 c. chopped pecans
1 t. salt
1 c. vegetable oil
4 eggs
3 c. grated carrots

Sift flour, soda and salt with cinnamon. Add oil, honey and eggs. Mix well. Fold in carrots, add nuts. Pour into 2 layer pans. Bake at 325° for 30 minutes or until done. Frost when cool, with:

8 oz. cream cheese   1 t. vanilla
⅓ c. honey

Cream cheese with honey and vanilla until smooth. Spread on cake.

HONEY HEALTH SHAKE

1 ripe banana
1 T. skim milk
1 T. brewers yeast
Juice of 1 fresh orange
1 T. honey
1 c. milk

Mix thoroughly in a blender until smooth and creamy.

SOFTENING ELBOW RUB

1 t. lemon juice
1 t. honey
1 t. cold pressed safflower oil

Dear Mr Parkhill,

After mentioning your book to a fellow honey-lover, we've found a remarkable difference in our family with weight loss, fewer allergy problems and no more hyper-8 yr. old, just to name a few.

Thank you for compiling it

Sincerely,
Linda Burns

Stone Mill Herbs
1381 Delaware Avenue
Buffalo, New York 14209

Dear Joe,

I am delighted with your "honey book" and enclose my check for 6 additional copies Please send them C.O.D.

Sincerely,
Sue Murray

OKLAHOMA'S GREATEST NEWSPAPER
TULSA WORLD

Dear Mr. Parkhill—

Help! We're drowning in requests for your address in connection with your book. Julie Blakely did a piece in the Family Section about your book. I had a letter from Susan Storch recommending it as "Summer Reading" and used it on the book page on Sunday, July 17. The results have been incredible.

With all good wishes,
Mildred Ladner
Book Editor

From the desk of
DAILEEN PLUMMER

Dear Joe Parkhill,

Thanks for compiling such a book As a novice, avid apa discovery of your book is highlights of the great th my way in 1979 I hope to many of your books

Sincerely,
Daileen Plummer

Food Section of the Globe Demo am most interested in your address and comment that the "Best Friend" book she has found— "The Wonderful World of Honey Cookbook" by Joe Parkhill

Enclosed is a stamped envelope

dorothy sanford

Dear Mr Parkhill

This past February I ordered one copy of your fine (didn't know it then, of course) cookbook **The Wonderful World of Honey**. My wife does all the baking for our family of six. She has several "honey" cookbooks that are sadly wanting and was not exactly enthused when I gave her the copy I'd ordered from you

Her first murmur of appreciation came upon reading the inscription to her, personally, from the author Well now! In the ensuing months she has come to have complete faith in your book, has tried dozens of items, and truly enjoys the related information scattered throughout She swaps hints with customers and brags on your book Then I'm forced to say I have none for sale

This must be remedied Enclosed is my check for $76 20 for the purchase and shipping of 12 copies of your choice book

Yours truly,
Dave Tozier

---

enjoys

truly appreciate the time, knowledge and energy it took to compile your book It must be rewarding to help others learn a better way I know it is for me
Thank you again.

Please send me:
- ☐ *The Wonderful World of Honey* at $6.95 ea. + .95 postage. ISBN-0-936744-01-4
- ☐ *Honey — God's Gift* at $6.95 ea. + .95 postage. ISBN-0-936744-02-2
- ☐ *Here's To You Honey* at $6.95 ea. + .95 postage. ISBN-0-936744-03-0
- ☐ *Nature's Golden Treasure* at $16.95 ea. + .95 postage. ISBN-0-936744-04-9
- ☐ *The No-Diet Way* at $6.95 ea. + .95 postage. ISBN-0-936744-00-6
- ☐ *The Wonderful World of Whey Lovers* at $6.95 ea. + .95 postage. ISBN-0-936744-08-1
- ☐ *The Wonderful World of Pollen* at $6.95 ea. + .95 postage. ISBN-0-936744-06-5
- ☐ *God Did Not Create Sickness & Disease* at $6.95 ea. + .95 postage. ISBN-0-936744-07-3

Canadian Residents Remit $7.95 + .95 postage.

Mail To:
Country Bazaar Publishing & Distributing
Route 2, Box 190 • Berryville, AR 72616
(501) 423-3131

ISBN-0-936744

Name _____

Address _____

City/State _____

Zip _____ Phone _____